LARGO E ALLEGRETT

Arranged for Oboe by
EVELYN ROTHWELL

BENEDETTO MARCELLO

LARGO

CH 01564

ALLEGRETTO
con eleganza e precisione ritmica

LARGO E ALLEGRETTO

Arranged by
EVELYN ROTHWELL

BENEDETTO MARCELLO

CHESTER MUSIC

OBOE — LARGO E ALLEGRETTO

Arranged by
EVELYN ROTHWELL

BENEDETTO MARCELLO

SELECTED MUSIC FOR
OBOE AND PIANO

ARNE *(arr. Rothwell)*	Pastorale
BACH *(arr. Rothwell)*	Adagio
BAKER	Cantilena
BERKELEY	Sonatina
BESOZZI *(arr. Rothwell)*	Sonata in C major
BONI *(arr. Rothwell)*	Sonata in G major
BOYCE *(arr. Rothwell)*	Gavotte and Gigue
ELLIOT	Three Pieces
FIELD *(arr. Rothwell)*	Nocturne
LE FLEMING	Air and Dance
GRIEG *(arr. Blake)*	Four Pieces
HANDEL *(arr. Rothwell)*	Air and Rondo
HOVLAND	Variations Op. 64
LOEILLET *(arr. Rothwell)*	Sonata in C major
MARAIS *(arr. Craxton)*	Three Old French Dances
MARCELLO *(arr. Rothwell)*	Largo and Allegretto
MORTHENSEN	Sonata
MOZART *(arr. Rothwell/Craxton)*	Oboe Quartet
MOZART *(arr. Rothwell)*	Two Songs
NICHOLAS	Two Pieces: Melody, Rhapsody
NIELSEN	Two Fantasy Pieces, Op. 2
POULENC	Sonata
RICHARDSON	Aria and Allegretto
SAMMARTINI *(arr. Rothwell)*	Sonata in G major
TESSARINI *(arr. Rothwell/Aveling)*	Sonata No 1 in F
THREE FRENCH PIECES *(arr. Rothwell):*	
Couperin	Le Bavolet Flottant
Dandrieu	Les Fifres
Rameau	Les Tendres Plaintes

From

CHESTER MUSIC

Exclusive distributors:
MUSIC SALES LIMITED
Newmarket Road, Bury St Edmunds,
Suffolk IP33 3YB

CHESTER MUSIC
part of The Music Sales Group
14–15 Berners Street, London W1T 3LJ, UK.

Exclusive distributors:
Music Sales Limited
Distribution Centre, Newmarket Road,
Bury St Edmunds, Suffolk IP33 3YB, UK.

www.chesternovello.com

CH01564

ISBN 978-0-7119-2271-6

9 780711 922716